WORLD'S MOST VALUABLE PLAYERS

Michael Heatley

PARKGATE
BOOKS

PRC Publishing Ltd,
Kiln House, 210 New Kings Road, London SW6 4NZ

This edition published in 1998 by
Parkgate Books Ltd
Kiln House
210 New Kings Road
London SW6 4NZ
Great Britain

© 1998 PRC Publishing Ltd

All rights reserved. No part of this publication may
be reproduced, stored in a retrieval system, or transmitted
in any form or by any means, electronic, mechanical,
photocopying, recording, or otherwise, without the prior
written permission of the Publisher and copyright holders.

British Library Cataloguing in Publication Data:
A catalogue record for this book is available from the British Library.

ISBN 1 90261 607 3

Printed and bound in China

Front cover: Ronaldo, (Above left), Owen (Above right), Bergkamp
(Below left), Shearer (Below right). *Allsport*

Back cover: Zidane. *Allsport*

Page 1: Suker. *Allsport*

Page 2: Ronaldo. *Shaun Botterill/Allsport*

WORLD'S MOST VALUABLE PLAYERS
CONTENTS

INTRODUCTION	4
GOALKEEPERS	6
DEFENDERS	18
MIDFIELDERS	44
STRIKERS	70
INDEX	96

WORLD'S MOST VALUABLE PLAYERS
INTRODUCTION

When Dwight Yorke became the second most expensive player in English football in August 1998 on his transfer from Aston Villa to Manchester United, it signalled the Old Trafford club's willingness to break the bank to reclaim the Premiership title they'd won in four of the previous six seasons.

As is the case these days, the club had to ask the permission of the plc that owns them before they spent the money – but with English football being played for the highest ever stakes, using satellite television money, and a European Superleague being covertly planned by United, Arsenal and other clubs, football was no place for the faint-hearted. Things had indeed changed in the four decades since 1958, when United's near-neighbours Bolton Wanderers won the FA Cup with a team of 11 men, none of whom had cost the club more than a £10 signing-on fee.

There were, of course, milestones on the way – such as the 1979 move that made Birmingham City forward Trevor Francis the first £1 million player when he moved to Nottingham Forest, like Manchester United today, at that time one of the top clubs in England. Now, Forest are among the Premiership's poor relations while Francis, back at Birmingham as manager, routinely adds £1 million-rated players to his squad even though the Blues are not yet in the top flight.

More complex is the Bosman ruling that allows players freedom of movement at the end of their contract if

Above: Manchester United's new £12.5m signing Dwight Yorke. *Allsport.*

Below: Trevor Francis the first British £1m player when he transferred from Birmingham City to Nottingham Forest in 1979. *Allsport.*

their current terms are not bettered. This has led to many big names moving on 'free transfers', the money the purchasing clubs save often ending up in the player's pocket in the form of signing-on fees, loyalty bonuses and/or simply wages. Some clubs have a rigid wage structure, while others allow their top players to have clauses in their contracts to ensure that their pay matches anyone brought in at a higher level of remuneration.

All of the above should tell you that, in attempting to name the 100 most valuable players in world football, this book has set itself an impossible task. Not only are top players changing colours weekly, but their notional fee often bears no relation to their actual value. When a player has one season of his contract left, clubs will often consider 'cashing in' and selling rather than waiting until the player can walk out 'on a Bosman', leaving his former employers with nothing but a blank space on the team-sheet.

Those who feel that the balance of power has tipped too far in the player's favour were given further fuel for thought when Dutchman Pierre van Hooijdonk went on strike on the eve of the 1998-99 season. He was unhappy at the lack of investment that his club, Nottingham Forest, had made in the transfer market and wanted away, less than half way through a four-year contract. That Forest acceded to his wishes seems to prove that contracts aren't worth the paper they're printed on – though Real Betis tried to warn off potential buyers with a £271 million release clause in Brazilian Denilson's contract when they purchased him for £21 million.

Whether or not you agree with our assessment of the world's 100 most valuable players, one thing's for certain – you'd have to break the bank, and then some, to buy this star-studded squad.

WORLD'S MOST VALUABLE PLAYERS
GOALKEEPERS

Fabien Barthez

Plays for: Monaco/France
Birthdate: 28 June 1971
Birthplace: Lavelanet, France
Joined club: 1995
Last transfer fee: £1.8 million
Current estimated value: £4 million

BARTHEZ

If the value of the French national team members doubled as a result of winning the 1998 World Cup, then a shutout against Brazil should have given Fabien Barthez's pricetag a welcome boost. Famous for the kiss Blanc gave him before every game, Barthez is cuddling up to supermodel Linda Evangelista off the pitch, but has performed well enough between the sticks for former club Marseille to make unsuccessful overtures about a return. Just 27, despite his lack of hair, he motivates his defenders by insulting them – and the rewards are there to see. Better not start that with Evangelista, though…

GOALKEEPERS

Jose Luis Chilavert

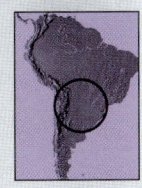

Plays for: Velez Sarsfield/Paraguay
Birthdate: 27 July 1965
Birthplace: Tucuman, Paraguay
Joined club: 1996
Last transfer fee: £2 million
Current estimated value: £3 million

CHILAVERT

With his penchant for roaming upfield to take penalties or even free-kicks around the edge of the area, Chilavert undoubtedly made himself the personality goalkeeper of France '98. Liverpool's abortive attempt to introduce him to the Premier League fell on deaf ears at Argentina's Velez Sarsfield, but at 33 he will now probably remain a South American phenomenon. National team captain.

Left: Fabien Barthez celebrates as France overcome Croatia 2-1 in the World Cup semi-finals. *Shaun Botterill/Allsport.*

Below: Chilavert seen in action for Paraguay in a World Cup qualifier against Argentina in 1996. *David Leah/Allsport.*

Above: Ruud Hesp in action in the European Super Cup against Borrusia Dortmund. *Shaun Botterill/Allsport.*

Right: Kasey Keller in goal for Leicester. *Graham Chadwick/Allsport.*

Ruud Hesp

Plays for: Barcelona/Holland
Birthdate: 31 October 1965
Birthplace: Bussum, Holland
Joined club: 1997
Last transfer fee: £1.4 million
Current estimated value: £3 million

Ruud Hesp would never have signed for Ajax, where Louis Van Gaal had national keeper Edwin Van Der Sar at his disposal. But when the coach moved to Barcelona in the summer of 1997, he returned home to pluck the promising Hesp from the unfashionable Roda JC. Though he'd just helped his team win the Cup, Hesp may have been motivated by the fact that they were possibly to merge with MVV and Fortuna Sittard, but there's little doubt he would have won the three-way battle of the keepers had the abortive move taken place. Now has Cocu and Zenden to keep him company at the Nou Camp.

GOALKEEPERS

Kasey Keller

Plays for: Leicester City/USA
Birthdate: 27 November 1969
Birthplace: Washington, USA
Joined club: 1996
Club League appearances: 63
Last transfer fee: £900,000
Current estimated value: £3 million

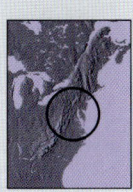

By stating his intention to end his playing career on the continent, Kasey Keller signalled that 1998-99 will be his last season at Filbert Street. There's little doubt that the Foxes' ability to avoid a speedy return to the Nationwide League as suffered by the likes of Palace, Bolton and Nottingham Forest in recent seasons has been aided by his commanding presence. A noted shot-stopper whose performance in USA's 1-0 win against Brazil won high praise from Romario.

Gianluca Pagliuca

Plays for: Inter Milan/Italy
Birthdate: 18 December 1966
Birthplace: Bologna, Italy
Joined club: 1994
Last transfer fee: - (part exchange deal)
Current estimated value: £3.5 million

Replacing friendly rival Peruzzi for 1997's Le Tournoi, Pagliuca let in five goals in two games – yet his club form had been strong and Maldini had no qualms letting him keep goal in France '98, adding a second World Cup to his curriculum vitae. A spectacular performer, it will be interesting to see how he fares under new national coach Dino Zoff, himself a goalkeeping legend.

Above: Juv's Angelo Peruzzi organises his wall during a Champions league match semi-final against Monaco.
Ben Radford/Allsport.

Left: Gianluca Pagliuca in a Serie A game against Padova.
Claudio Villa/Allsport.

Angelo Peruzzi

Plays for: Juventus/Italy
Birthdate: 16 February 1970
Birthplace: Viterbo, Italy
Joined club: 1991
Last transfer fee: Not disclosed
Current estimated value: £4.5 million

The Number 1 choice for his country before France '98, having impressed English crowds with a shut-out performance in February 1997's Wembley qualifying clash, Peruzzi was unfortunate to pick up an injury and lose out to Pagliuca, four years his senior. Nevertheless, his performances have helped Juventus dominate Italian football and at 28 he has time to contemplate another World Cup.

Above: Peter Schmeichel in usual vocal mood in a FA Carling Premier game versus Leeds in September 1997. *Allsport*

Right: David Seaman proudly holds aloft the FA Carling Premiership trophy. *Shaun Botterill/Allsport.*

Peter Schmeichel

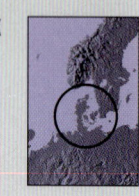

Plays for: Manchester United/Denmark
Birthdate: 18 November 1963
Birthplace: Gladsaxe, Denmark
Joined club: 1991
Club League appearances: 258
Last transfer fee: £550,000
Current estimated value: £5 million

Manchester United's record of four Premiership wins in five years is testament to the consistency and commanding presence of their last line of defence. Schmeichel arrived at Old Trafford in 1991, the year before his country's surprise European Championship win, and proceeded to prove remarkable value for money by filling what had always been the Red Devils' problem position. His mastery of angles is complete, and few forwards beat him in one-on-one situations.

GOALKEEPERS

David Seaman

Plays for: Arsenal/England
Birthdate: 19 September 1963
Birthplace: Rotherham
Joined club: 1990
Club League appearances: 280
Last transfer fee: £1.3 million
Current estimated value: £3.5 million

It was a long, hard climb to the top for David Seaman, whose career looked bound for journeyman status in the lower divisions when he was released by first club Leeds in 1982. He has had the last laugh of course, arriving at Highbury via Peterborough, Birmingham and QPR and establishing himself as first choice for the Double winners as well as England. Though Arsenal may cash in due to the presence of capable reserve Alex Manninger, Seaman still has several seasons left at the top and may well emulate predecessor Pat Jennings in longevity terms.

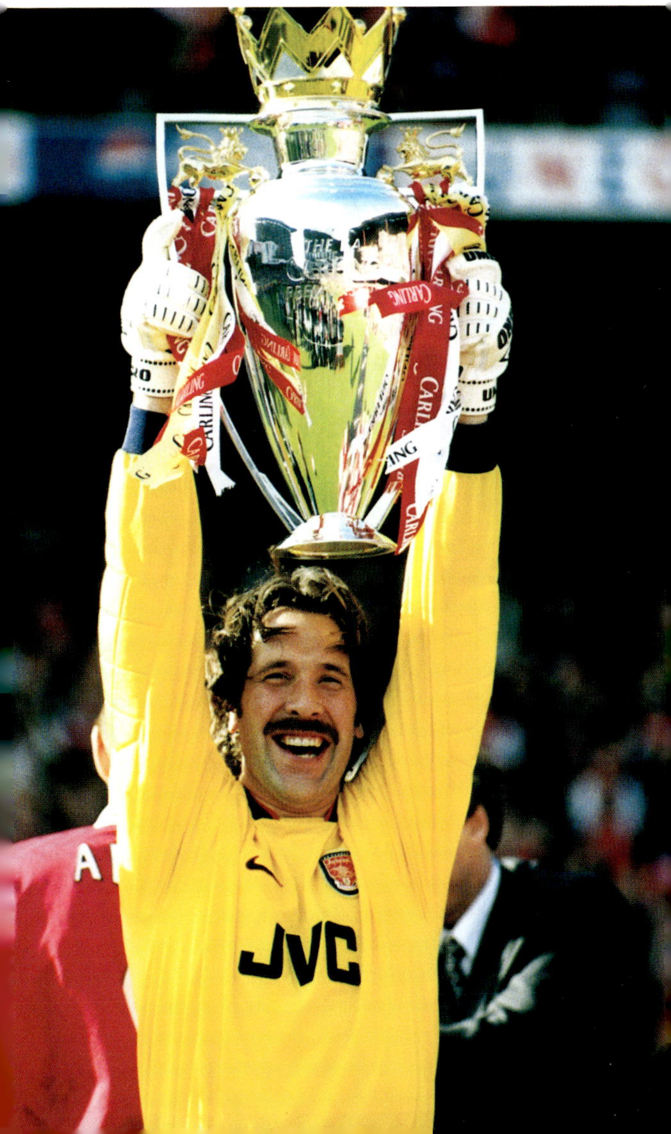

Steve Simonsen

Plays for: Tranmere Rovers/England
Birthdate: 3 April 1979
Birthplace: South Shields
Joined club: 1996
Club League appearances: 30
Current estimated value: £4 million

SIMONSEN

In historical terms, Tranmere Rovers is hardly the breeding ground for young keepers: both Tommy Lawrence (Liverpool) and Gordon West (Everton) ended their careers 'over the water'. But this superb young prospect, hitherto unblooded in League action, took the Number 1 jersey in November 1997 from Danny Coyne and held it for an unbroken 30-game run that saw the Prenton Park club claw their way from the relegation zone to a respectable 14th place. Six clean sheets over Christmas/New Year marked Simonsen as a man to watch, and Everton's £4 million bid was on the table as the 1998-99 season started.

GOALKEEPERS

Above: Claudio Taffarel during an international friendly against Germany. *Mark Thompson/Allsport.*

Left: Steve Simonsen of Tramere Rovers. *Allsport.*

Claudio Taffarel

Plays for: Galatasaray/Brazil
Birthdate: 8 May 1966
Birthplace: Santa Rosa, Brazil
Joined club: 1998
Last transfer fee: £435,000
Current estimated value: £3.5 million

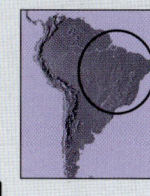

TAFFAREL

In Brazil, no-one wants to be a goalkeeper – but Claudio Taffarel's match-winning performance in the 1994 World Cup Final may have made some converts. An extra-time save at Roberto Baggio's feet took the goalless tie to penalties, and a save from Massaro's spot-kick in the penalty shoot-out psyched out Baggio once again. Had a competent tournament in '98, following which Faith Terim took him to Galatasaray for a remarkably low fee.

Above: Edwin Van der Sar representing Holland.
Alex Liversey/Allsport.

Right: Vitor Baia shouting instructions to his defence.
Laurence Griffiths/Allsport.

Edwin Van der Sar

Plays for: Ajax/Holland
Birthdate: 29 October 1970
Birthplace: Voorhout, Holland
Joined club: 1987
Current estimated value: £4 million

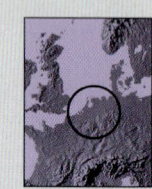

VAN der SAR

The only member of Holland's 1998 World Cup squad to still be playing his football in the Netherlands (excluding the on-strike de Boer twins) as the 1998-99 season kicked off, Van der Sar is nothing if not consistent. Began the 1995-96 season with nine clean sheets, confirming his command of the Ajax Number 1 position since the demise of Stanley Menzo. Supplanted Ed De Goey in the national team and his calm, unhurried demeanour suggests that he'll stay there.

GOALKEEPERS

Vitor Baia

Plays for: Barcelona/Portugal
Birthdate: 15 October 1969
Birthplace: Sao Pedro Afurada, Portugal
Joined club: 1996
Last transfer fee: £3 million
Current estimated value: £3 million

BAIA

Portugal's long-established national keeper transferred from Champions Porto to Spanish giants Barcelona in summer 1996, following coach Bobby Robson. He missed only one game as the Nou Camp side came in second in 1996-97, but incoming boss Louis Van Gaal brought in fellow countryman Ruud Hesp as last line of defence, prompting a battle for the Number 1 jersey.

WORLD'S MOST VALUABLE PLAYERS
DEFENDERS

Tony Adams

Plays for: Arsenal/England
Birthdate: 10 October 1966
Birthplace: London
Joined club: 1984
Club League appearances: 421
Club League goals: 30
Current estimated value: £3.5 million

Having battled with much-publicised personal problems, Tony Adams now sees every season as a bonus – and far from finding his place under threat in the Arsène Wenger regime, he's added to his all-round game by acquiring an unsuspected urge to come forward with the ball and take up attacking positions.

DEFENDERS

Slaven Bilic

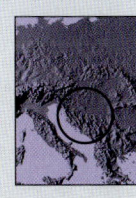

Plays for: Everton/Croatia
Birthdate: 11 September 1968
Birthplace: Split, Croatia
Joined club: 1997
Club League appearances: 24
Last transfer fee: £4.5 million
Current estimated value: £4.5 million

Though he suffered at the hands of the press – and home fans – when his histrionics had Laurent Blanc sent off in the World Cup semi-final, Slaven Bilic remains a rugged, dependable defender whose performances in France (that moment of madness apart) confirmed his world-class status. Formed a solid central defensive partnership for his country with Derby's Stimac, but his place at Everton, where he's set to play alongside Italian youngster Marco Materazzi, must be consolidated under new manager Walter Smith.

Left: Arsenal and England captain Tony Adams.
Shaun Botterill/Allsport.

Below: Slaven Bilic shares a joke with Newcastle's Alan Shearer,*/Allsport.*

Cafu

Plays for: Roma/Brazil
Birthdate: 7 June 1970
Birthplace: Sao Paulo, Brazil
Joined club: 1997
Last transfer fee: £3.5 million
Current estimated value: £4 million

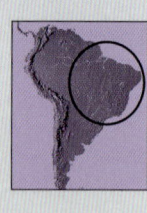

The summer of 1997 saw Roma respond to a dire 12th place with a wholesale change of players, encouraging right-back Marco de Moraes Cafu to make the move from Palmeiras in his native Brazil to play alongside the likes of countrymate Aldair and Austrian star Konsel in the Italian capital. Cafu and Aldair linked again in the national team in France '98, though the former was out for the semi-final due to suspension and was much missed.

Above: Tottenham and England defender Sol Campbell. *Shaun Botterill/Allsport.*

Left: Cafu in Brazilian colours. *Mark Thompson/Allsport.*

Sol Campbell

Plays for: Tottenham Hotspur/England
Birthdate: 18 September 1974
Birthplace: Newham
Joined club: 1992
Club League appearances: 168
Club League goals: 2
Current estimated value: £8 million

The highlight of a dismal few years for Tottenham fans has been the emergence of a new defensive star as cultured as he is commanding. A home-grown prospect, Campbell's place in the England back four is assured barring injury for a decade to come, but there'll be no-one surprised if he should ply his trade in Serie A should Spurs continue in the domestic doldrums.

21

Above: Roberto Carlos of Real Madrid and Brazil during the World Cup Final. *Ben Radford/Allsport.*

Right: Frank de Boer in Dutch colours. *Graham Chadwick/Allsport.*

Roberto Carlos

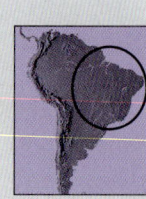

Plays for: Real Madrid/Brazil
Birthdate: 10 April 1973
Birthplace: Sao Paulo
Joined club: 1996
Last transfer fee: £3 million
Current estimated value: £5 million

CARLOS

After unleashing a famous curving free-kick against France in 1997's Le Tournoi, Roberto Carlos was unable to repeat the feat in the following year's World Cup. Even so, he was part of the Real Madrid team that won the European Cup weeks earlier – proof that his reputation (and future, since he is still just 25) remains rosy.

DEFENDERS

Frank de Boer

Plays for: Ajax/Holland
Birthdate: 15 May 1970
Birthplace: Hoorn, Holland
Joined club: 1989
Current estimated value: £4.5 million

A decade at Ajax seemed likely to end as Frank de Boer, along with his twin brother Ronald, resorted to law to escape long-term contracts (he lost his case, but refused to train). Certainly, an eight-year veteran of his country's defence who's still only 28 would attract the interest of the world's top clubs – especially since Frank's skill with the dead ball gives his game an attacking dimension. Missed Euro '96 through injury.

Marcel Desailly

Plays for: Chelsea/France
Birthdate: 7 September 1968
Birthplace: Accra, Ghana
Joined club: 1998
Last transfer fee: £5 million
Current estimated value: £5 million

DESAILLY

African-born but French in international terms, Marcel Desailly played his part with some coolly cultured displays in his adopted country's World Cup win. By this time he had become a Chelsea player, AC Milan letting him go for a £5 million fee, and he looked to rekindle his partnership in central defence with Frank Leboeuf, who'd deputised for Blanc in the Final (which Desailly missed after dismissal in the semis).

Above: Young Rio Ferdinand of West Ham and England. *Alex Liversey/Allsport.*

Left: World Cup winner Marcel Desailly. *Allsport.*

Rio Ferdinand

Plays for: West Ham United/England
Birthdate: 7 November 1978
Birthplace: London
Joined club: 1995
Club League appearances: 51
Club League goals: 2
Current estimated value: £3.5 million

France '98 came a little early for Rio Ferdinand, but England coach Glenn Hoddle had already blooded a player who looks the nearest the Hammers have found to a new Bobby Moore. Over the next decade, he seems certain to eclipse the 17 international caps won by cousin Les of Spurs, and his confidence on the ball can only increase. A certainty for Euro 2000.

Above: Vergard Heggam in a pre-season friendly./*Allsport*.

Right: Thomas Helveg in action for Denmark. *Shaun Botterill/Allsport*.

Vegard Heggem

Plays for: West Ham United/Norway
Birthdate: 7 November 1978
Birthplace: Norway
Joined club: 1995
Club League appearances: 51
Club League goals: 2
Current estimated value: £3.5 million

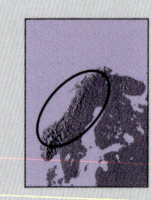

Right-sided defender with a penchant for the attacking wing-back role whose post-World Cup move in the summer of 1998 saw him join countrymen Leonhardsen, Kvarme and Bjornebye at Anfield. Two successful years in the Rosenborg side included a dramatic winning goal in the San Siro Stadium against Milan in the Champions League, so will not be overawed by the Anfield atmosphere.

DEFENDERS

Thomas Helveg

Plays for: AC Milan/Denmark
Birthdate: 24 June 1971
Birthplace: Kiel, Germany
Joined club: 1998
Last transfer fee: £5 million
Current estimated value: £5 million

HELVEG

Made his name in the Danish Superliga with OB Odense and was Denmark's Footballer of the Year for 1993-94. Midway through that season he was loaned to Italian club Udinese and, although the Friuli side were relegated, Helveg stayed to help them win instant promotion back to Serie A. Three seasons later, he followed Udinese coach Alberto Zaccheroni to AC Milan. Hard-working and versatile, Helveg is equally at ease playing as a man-marking defender or as a midfield anchorman.

Colin Hendry

Plays for: Rangers/Scotland
Birthdate: 7 December 1965
Birthplace: Keith
Joined club: 1998
Last transfer fee: £4 million
Current estimated value: £4 million

Having inspired his fellow Bravehearts in France '98, Scotland captain Colin Hendry found himself the subject of a transfer tussle as the new season approached. Blackburn's £5.5 million valuation was based as much on his leadership qualities as his playing ability, and Dick Advocaat saw him as the man to weld together Rangers' team of all nations whose defensive shortcomings were cruelly exposed by Hearts and Irish no-hopers Shelbourne even before September had been reached.

Above: Graeme Le Saux of Chelsea and England.
Stu Forster/Allsport.

Left: Scotland's Braveheart Colin Hendry.
Ben Radford/Allsport.

Graeme Le Saux

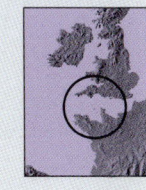

Plays for: Chelsea/England
Birthdate: 17 October 1968
Birthplace: Jersey
Joined club: 1997
Club League appearances: 26
Club League goals: 1
Last transfer fee: £5 million
Current estimated value: £5.5 million

Graeme Le Saux's return to Chelsea, having spent a title-winning spell with Blackburn from 1993, was unexpected given that he's a rare Englishman (albeit a Channel Islander) in the Stamford Bridge squad. Like full-back partner Petrescu, he is better coming forward than defending, but the Romanian enjoyed a far better World Cup. At 30, he is unlikely to feature in Euro 2000.

Above: Another Chelsea World Cup winner Frank Leboeuf seen in action against Crystal Palace. *Allsport.*

Right: AC Milan's Paolo Maldini. *Claudio Villa/Allsport.*

Frank Leboeuf

Plays for: Chelsea/France
Birthdate: 22 January 1968
Birthplace: Marseille, France
Joined club: 1996
Club League appearances: 58
Club League goals: 11
Last transfer fee: £2.5 million
Current estimated value: £3 million

Tall centre-back Leboeuf took full advantage of Laurent Blanc's semi-final dismissal to play a commanding role in France's World Cup win – then found himself wooed by Liverpool. Yet the possibility of recreating the partnership with Desailly at Stamford Bridge won out and he stayed put – and after four medals in two seasons (FA Cup, League Cup, European Cup Winners' Cup and World Cup) he was clearly on a roll.

DEFENDERS

Paolo Maldini

Plays for: AC Milan/Italy
Birthdate: 26 June 1968
Birthplace: Milan
Joined club: 1985
Current estimated value: £7 million

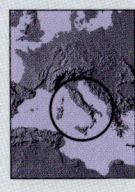

MALDINI

A one-club man, Paolo Maldini's place in the AC Milan and Italy sides is almost taken for granted – even if his father retired after a disappointing World Cup. Maldini Junior's taken on the mantle of Franco Baresi in the blue shirt with few problems, though life with Milan has been somewhat rockier. At 30, will aim to contest another World Cup.

Miguel Nadal

Plays for: Barcelona/Spain
Birthdate: 28 July 1966
Birthplace: Mallorca
Joined club: 1991
Last transfer fee: £800,000
Current estimated value: £4 million

NADAL

Many believe Manchester United's Alex Ferguson settled for an expensive second best when he bought Jaap Stam rather than the man who'd headed his defensive shopping list for a season – Miguel Angel Nadal. He rarely hits the headlines, but with the departure of Ferrer to Chelsea is one of the few Spaniards left at the Nou Camp. Flourished under Johan Cruyff, playing 'total football' in a variety of positions before national coach Javier Clemente introduced him to the sweeper position which he now occupies with aplomb.

Above: Morocco's Nourredine Naybet.
Clive Brunskill/Allsport.

Left: Barcelona's Miguel Nadal in action against Newcastle in the Champions League. *Stu Forster/Allsport.*

Nourredine Naybet

Plays for: Deportivo La Coruna/Morocco
Birthdate: 10 February 1970
Birthplace: Casablanca, Morocco
Joined club: 1997
Last transfer fee: £1 million
Current estimated value: £4 million

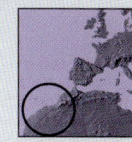

Morocco may not be a world footballing force, but Nourredine Naybet, their best-known player, certainly deserves a major stage. Still just 28, his total of international caps will shortly enter three figures, but his club Deportivo's slip from third to 12th will not please him. Played in all three of his country's World Cup group games, but the chance of a last big-money move may have eluded him.

Above: Gary Neville lines up for Manchester United in a Champions League match versus FC Kosice

Right: Dutch Midfielder Arthur Numan.
Alex Liversey/Allsport.

Gary Neville

Plays for: Manchester United/England
Birthdate: 18 February 1975
Birthplace: Bury
Joined club: 1993
Club League appearances: 115
Club League goals: 1
Current estimated value: £7 million

The elder of Manchester United's two defender brothers continues to impress quietly, his ability to play at right-back or centrally making him an invaluable squad member for both club and country. Injury permitting, the local boy looks good for another decade at the top, and odds are that will be at United.

DEFENDERS

Arthur Numan

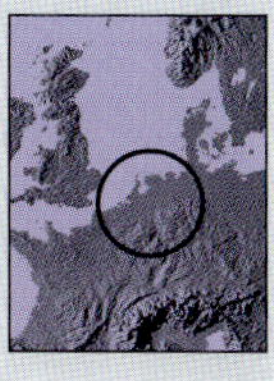

Plays for: Rangers/Holland
Birthdate: 14 December 1969
Birthplace: Heemskerk, Holland
Joined club: 1998
Last transfer fee: £5 million
Current estimated value: £5 million

When former Dutch international coach Dick Advocaat slipped into the Rangers managerial chair, his first move was to claim the services of a player he knew well. Left-back Numan appeared to adapt well to life in a new country, his arrival freeing up Jorg Albertz to take an attacking midfield role. Unlucky to be sent off in World Cup against Argentina.

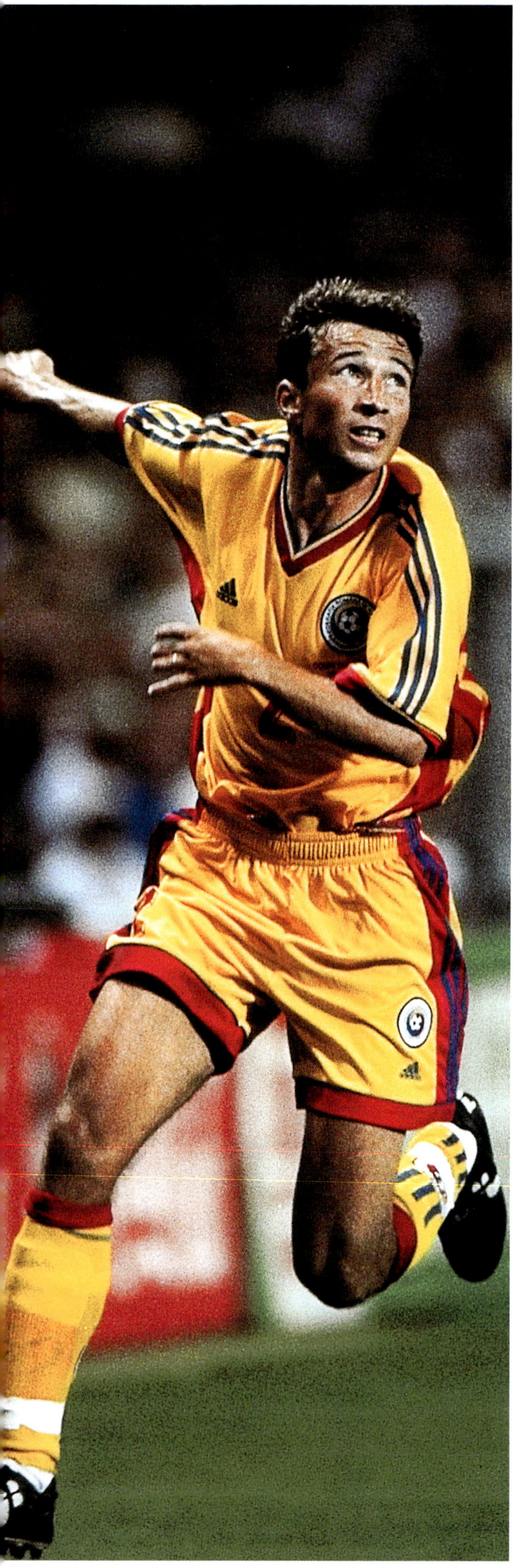

Dan Petrescu

Plays for: Chelsea/Romania
Birthdate: 22 December 1967
Birthplace: Bucharest, Romania
Joined club: 1995
Club League appearances: 89
Club League goals: 10
Last transfer fee: £2.3 million
Current estimated value: £3.5 million

Sheffield Wednesday nearly doubled their money by selling attack-minded full-back Dan Petrescu to Chelsea after little more than one season, and many thought Ruud Gullit had paid over the odds. Yet his arrival in November 1995 coincided with an upturn in fortunes that won the club three trophies in two seasons. His dismissal in the 1998 Cup Winners' Cup Final was unfortunate, but appearing in his second World Cup was some consolation. Rumoured to be on the move in late 1998.

Left: Dan Petrescu of Romania and Chelsea in World Cup action against England. *Allsport*.

Tomas Repka

Plays for: Fiorentina/Czech Republic
Birthdate: 2 January 1974
Birthplace: Ostrava, Czech Republic
Joined club: 1998
Last transfer fee: £4.8 million
Current estimated value: £4.8 million

A versatile performer who can play right wing-back or centrally, Repka helped Sparta Prague to the Czech Championship in 1997 and 1998 before beating a well-worn path abroad. Made his international debut for the old RCS when still at Banik Ostrava, and should remain a fixture in the Czech rearguard while in Serie A.

Above: Gareth Southgate of Aston Villa seen playing against Notts County FA Cup third round. *Mark Thompson/Allsport.*

Right: £10.75m defender Jaap Stam. *Ben Radford/Allsport.*

Gareth Southgate

Plays for: Aston Villa/England
Birthdate: 3 September 1970
Birthplace: Watford
Joined club: 1995
Club League appearances: 91
Club League goals: 2
Last transfer fee: £2.5 million
Current estimated value: £4.5 million

Forever damned as the player who missed the vital penalty in the Euro '96 semi-final, Southgate has shrugged off that disappointment to prove adept at preventing goals rather than attempting them. Injury disrupted his 1998 World Cup, though he'd played his part in turning Villa's disastrous domestic season into a late dash for Europe. May find future international opportunities limited by younger rivals Campbell and Ferdinand.

DEFENDERS

Jaap Stam

Plays for: Manchester United/Holland
Birthdate: 17 July 1972
Birthplace: Kampen, Holland
Joined club: 1998
Last transfer fee: £10.75 million
Current estimated value: £10.75 million

Looked ponderous when faced with the world's best in France '98, but six-footer Stam was unused to the spotlight having become the most expensive defender ever weeks earlier in moving from PSV to Manchester United. The Premiership's move away from long-ball to continental style may make his life more difficult yet, but he has great timing in the tackle for a big man and could still have the last laugh.

Moreno Torricelli

Plays for: Fiorentina/Italy
Birthdate: 23 January 1970
Birthplace: Alessandria, Italy
Joined club: 1998
Last transfer fee: £4 million
Current estimated value: £4 million

After six years' loyal service to Juventus, this uncompromising, no-nonsense wing-back moved to Fiorentina in the summer of 1998. During his time with Juve he won the Italian Double in 1995 and the European Cup a year later – although his career was also dogged with niggling injuries, some of them no doubt caused by his unwillingness to pull out of a tackle!

DEFENDERS

Above: Taribo West in Nigerian colours, hair as well!
Shaun Botterill/Allsport.

Left: Former Juventus defender Torricelli.
Ben Radford/Allsport.

Taribo West

Plays for: Inter Milan/Nigeria
Birthdate: 26 March 1974
Birthplace: Port Harcourt, Nigeria
Joined club: 1997
Last transfer fee: £3.5 million
Current estimated value: £4.5 million

With his colourful hairstyle, the imposing West made a visual mark on France '98 – and his play impressed Liverpool enough to table a £6 million bid, rejected by the player who preferred to remain with Baggio, Ronaldo and Djorkaeff in an attractive Inter team. Idolised at the San Siro with 'Taribo eats you up!' banners, he first made his name at Auxerre.

Christian Wörns

Plays for: Paris Saint Germain/Germany
Birthdate: 10 May 1972
Birthplace: Mannheim, Germany
Joined club: 1998
Last transfer fee: £4.5 million
Current estimated value: £4.5 million

Wörns

Playing for unfashionable Bayer 04 Leverkusen, Wörns played a major role (with striker Ulf Kirsten) in sending them to second place in 1996-97's Bundesliga, relighting his international ambitions after becoming becalmed on eight caps. UEFA Cup experience added to his game, Berti Vogts restored him to the German team for France '98 and, after failing in their bid to land Taribo West, Liverpool turned their attention to him. Instead, he preferred to remain with French Cup winners PSG.

Below: Christian Wörns goes past Mehdi Pashazadeh of Iran in a World Cup group match. *Shaun Botterill/Allsport.*

WORLD'S MOST VALUABLE PLAYERS

MIDFIELDERS

David Beckham

Plays for: Manchester United/England
Birthdate: 2 May 1975
Birthplace: Leytonstone
Joined club: 1993
Club League appearances: 110
Club League goals: 23
Current estimated value: £10 million

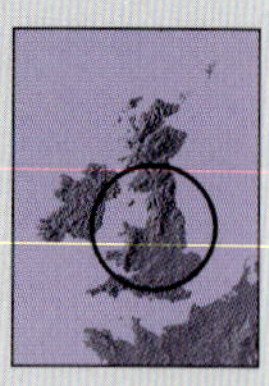

The meteoric rise of Manchester United's most inventive midfielder was halted by that rash challenge in the World Cup against Argentina – but should he show the character to weather the storm, the sky, and ultimately one suspects Serie A, is the limit. Accuracy with the dead ball is legendary, but can still fade out of games.

MIDFIELDERS

Rui Costa

Plays for: Fiorentina/Portugal
Birthdate: 29 March 1972
Birthplace: Lisbon, Portugal
Joined club: 1994
Last transfer fee: £5 million
Current estimated value: £5 million

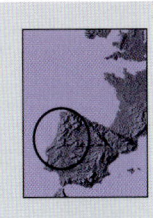

COSTA

During the summer of 1994, no foreign player arrived in Italy with a higher price-tag on his head than Rui Manuel Cesar Costa. The £5 million ticket seemed high for a 22 year old with only three years' first-team experience at Benfica, but over the next four years Rui Costa proved a consistently effective foil for Fiorentina striker Gabriel Batistuta, earning the nickname 'the new Antognoni'. Has been a regular Portuguese international since 1993.

Left: Manchester United's David Beckham in England colours. *Ross Kinnaird/Allsport.*

Below: Rui Costa of Fiorentina. *Claudio Villa/Allsport.*

Edgar Davids

Plays for: Juventus/Holland
Birthdate: 13 March 1973
Birthplace: Amsterdam, Holland
Joined club: 1998
Last transfer fee: £3.4 million
Current estimated value: £6 million

Having fallen out with national coach Hiddink in Euro '96, terrier-like Davids made his mark on France '98, allegedly becoming the player with the most free-kicks against his name. Absolutely vital to the national effort, but needs to add goalscoring to his game to become the complete player and worthy of his 'new Ruud Gullit' tag.

Above: Ajax's Ronald de Boer in Dutch colours. *Alex Livesey/Allsport.*

Left: Edgar Davids in World Cup action. *Allsport.*

Ronald de Boer

Plays for: Ajax/Holland
Birthdate: 15 May 1970
Birthplace: Hoorn, Holland
Joined club: 1993
Current estimated value: £5 million

de BOER

The more creative of the de Boer twins, Ronald (who spent two years away from Ajax In 1991-93 with Twente) is now seeking a new challenge, having been two decades with the Dutch giants as man and boy. Having played up front, he knows where to make his trademark runs to pose maximum threat, and at 28 is the complete player in his prime.

Above: Ivan de la Peña in Barcelona's Cup Winners Cup win. *Allsport.*

Right: Denilson in an international friendly against Germany. *David Cannon/Allsport.*

Ivan de la Peña

Plays for: Lazio/Spain
Birthdate: 6 May 1976
Birthplace: Santander, Spain
Joined club: 1998
Last transfer fee: £10 million
Current estimated value: £10 millionn

de la PENA

Signed on a £3.5 million a year contract from Barcelona, the 'bad boy' of the Nou Camp never saw eye to eye with Barca's Dutch coach Louis van Gaal during the 1997-98 season. Was so glad to arrive at Lazio that he called on his former Barcelona team-mate Ronaldo to join him there – and Serie A should be a fitting stage for his elegant, long-passing game. Was controversially left out of Spain's squad for Euro '96, and sadly his lack of first-team football also ruled him out of France '98.

MIDFIELDERS

Denilson

Plays for: Real Betis/Brazil
Birthdate: 24 August 1977
Birthplace: Sao Paolo, Brazil
Joined club: 1998
Last transfer fee: £22 million
Current estimated value: £22 million

The world's most expensive footballer only became a Betis player six months after signing the deal that saw a world-record cheque for £22 million winging its way from Seville to Sao Paulo. Ambitious Betis president has gambled his club's entire future on the pacy left-sided forward, even recruiting a Portuguese-speaking coach – Antonio Oliveira – to get the best from him. Seldom got the chance to shine at France '98, but don't let that fool you.

Didier Deschamps

Plays for: Juventus/France
Birthdate: 15 October 1968
Birthplace: Bayonne, France
Joined club: 1994
Current estimated value: £5 million

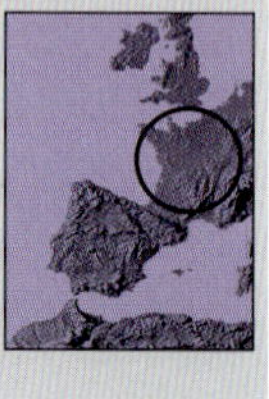

DESCHAMPS

The man Eric Cantona once dubbed a 'water carrier' has now boarded the winner's rostrum to lift both the European Cup and the World Cup as team captain. France's World Cup win was only the latest in a line of accolades which includes European Cup success with Marseille in 1993 and with Juventus three years later. He is a supreme winner and distributor of the ball.

Above: Roberto Di Matteo tussles with Lee Hendrie of Aston Villa. *Allsport.*

Left: Didier Deschamps holds aloft the World Cup. *David Leah/Allsport.*

Roberto Di Matteo

Plays for: Chelsea/Italy
Birthdate: 29 May 1970
Birthplace: Schaffhausen, Switzerland
Joined club: 1996
Club League appearances: 64
Club League goals: 11
Last transfer fee: £4.9 million
Current estimated value: £5 millionn

The only English-based Italian to be selected for World Cup '98 duty, Di Matteo's two years at Chelsea have seen the club garner three trophies. Yet his stated intention to return to Italy at some future point has never let fans regard him as 'their own'. His all-round abilities, including ball-winning and striking from deep, make this Swiss-born ace a valuable performer whether in the Premiership or Serie A.

Above: Ryan Giggs in full stride. *Shaun Botterill/Allsport.*

Right: Brazilian international Giovanni.
Ben Radford/Allsport.

Ryan Giggs

Plays for: Manchester United/Wales
Birthdate: 29 November 1973
Birthplace: Cardiff
Joined club: 1990
Club League appearances: 236
Club League goals: 50
Current estimated value: £10 million

Like Ian Rush and Mark Hughes, Giggs has suffered through representing a country unable to qualify for the finals of major tournaments – yet his success on the biggest club stage available with Manchester United is some consolation. The arrival of Jesper Blomqvist at Old Trafford in 1998 saw Giggs move into central midfield – an indication of manager Alex Ferguson's belief that his prodigious talent has now fully matured.

MIDFIELDERS

Giovanni

Plays for: Barcelona/Brazil
Birthdate: 4 February 1972
Birthplace: Belen, Brazil
Joined club: 1996
Last transfer fee: £4.25 million
Current estimated value: £22 million

GIOVANNI

Signed from Santos in the summer of 1996, Giovanni infuriated the then Barca boss Bobby Robson with his lack of discipline on and off the pitch, but went on to supply some powerful ammunition for striker Ronaldo, as well as scoring some goals of his own. Now in his third season at the Nou Camp, he was a member of Brazil's 1998 World Cup squad but was dropped after the tournament opener against Scotland.

Jorg Heinrich

Plays for: Fiorentina/Germany
Birthdate: 6 December 1969
Birthplace: Rathenow, Germany
Joined club: 1998
Last transfer fee: £5 million
Current estimated value: £5 million

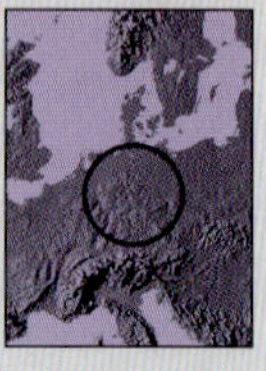

HEINRICH

Signed from Borussia Dortmund in the summer of '98, Heinrich was one of the few bright spots of Germany's ill-fated World Cup campaign in France. A flexible midfielder who can play wide as well as through the middle, he was a German title winner with Dortmund in 1996 and won the European Cup with them a year later. A native of the former German Democratic Republic, he cut his teeth in the GDR's Oberliga and then with SC Freiburg in the Bundesliga.

Above: Michael Owen and Paul Ince celebrate in a pre-season friendly. *Clive Brunskill/Allsport.*

Left: Jorg Heinrich in Borrussia Dortmund Colours. *Ben Radford/Allsport.*

Paul Ince

Plays for: Liverpool/England
Birthdate: 21 October 1967
Birthplace: Ilford
Joined club: 1997
Club League appearances: 31
Club League goals: 8
Last transfer fee: £4.2 million
Current estimated value: £5 million

A natural captain and midfield ball-winner, Paul Ince seemed the final piece in the Championship jigsaw for Liverpool when he returned from Serie A duty with Inter Milan in the summer of 1997. It didn't work out that way, but having tasted success in five years at Old Trafford he remains hungry for more – and the way the Kop have taken the ex-Mancunian who started life at West Ham to heart proves they know it. An England fixture and cert for Euro 2000.

Above: Juninho in action for Athletico Madrid against Leicester in the UEFA Cup. *Ben Radford/Allsport.*

Right: Brian Laudrup in action for Rangers. *Clive Brunskill/Allsport.*

Juninho

Plays for: Atletico Madrid/Brazil
Birthdate: 22 February 1973
Birthplace: Sao Paolo, Brazil
Joined club: 1997
Last transfer fee: £12 million
Current estimated value: £12 million

Aston Villa failed in their £12 million attempt to bring this mercurial performer back to the Premiership in summer 1998 – a shame, since his creative midfield displays for Middlesbrough remain a happy memory for all who saw them. Had poor luck in Spain, where he broke his ankle and was omitted from Brazil's squad even though he claimed to have recovered.

MIDFIELDERS

Brian Laudrup

Plays for: Chelsea/Denmark
Birthdate: 22 February 1969
Birthplace: Vienna, Austria
Joined club: 1998
Current estimated value: £5 million

LAUDRUP

Acclaimed as one of Rangers' best ever buys, Danish international Brian Laudrup did enough in France '98 to suggest that Chelsea had done well to tempt him to Stamford Bridge under the Bosman ruling. Prefers to play wide rather than centrally, but his versatility may serve him well in a large squad where no-one can be sure of their place. Now in his late 20s, he has retired from international football, which could be bad news for Premiership full-backs in 1998-99.

Steve McManaman

Plays for: Liverpool/England
Birthdate: 11 February 1972
Birthplace: Liverpool
Joined club: 1990
Club League appearances: 244
Club League goals: 42
Current estimated value: £10 million

The 1998-99 season looked crucial for swift-dribbling Steve McManaman, who failed to secure a place in England's midfield in France and had also been subject of transfer speculation the previous season when Barcelona made a move. It was disappointing given his ever-present England status in Euro '96 and suggested more application was necessary to ensure that his long-evident talent (he made his debut in 1990, aged 18) was exploited to the full.

Above: Jay-Jay Okocha of Nigeria. *Ross Kinnaird/Allsport.*

Left: Liverpool winger Steve McManaman. *Phil Cole/Allsport.*

Jay-Jay Okocha

Plays for: Paris Saint Germain/Nigeria
Birthdate: 14 August 1973
Birthplace: Ilorin, Kwara State
Joined club: 1998
Club League appearances: —
Club League goals: —
Last transfer fee: £11.2 million
Current estimated value: £11.2 million

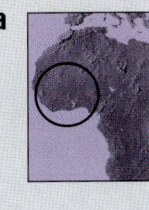

Having played football in Germany and Turkey, as well as impressed for his country in the 1994 USA World Cup, Nigeria's Okocha added another page to his footballing passport when he moved to Paris Saint Germain in summer 1998. Real name Austin, he really motors in midfield and has no fears about following Brazilians Rai and Leonardo at PSG. Pace, ball control and a powerful, unpredictable shot have made him a crowd pleaser wherever he goes, even though national team colleagues were not unanimous in their praise. Currently sports a red thatch.

Above: Ariel Ortega headbutts Dutch keeper Edwin Van der Sar. *Ben Radford/Allsport.*

Right: Mark Overmars in the FA Cup final. *Allsport.*

Ariel Ortega

Plays for: Sampdoria/Argentina
Birthdate: 4 March 1974
Birthplace: Libertador General San Martin, Argentina
Joined club: 1998
Last transfer fee: £4.8 million
Current estimated value: £6 million

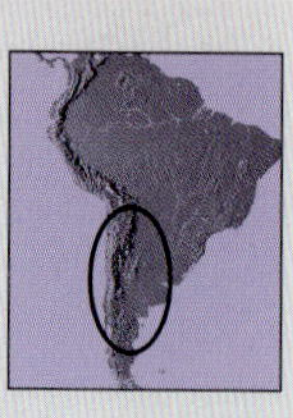

Ariel Ortega personifies the philosophy of national manager Daniel Passarella — a midfielder who can defend impressively yet attack with pace. Linked impressively with Italian-based Veron and Simeone in France '98 but his fiery temperament, as displayed by his World Cup sending-off for a headbutt against Holland, will be under scrutiny in Serie A this season following his summer move from Valencia.

MIDFIELDERS

Marc Overmars

Plays for: Arsenal/Holland
Birthdate: 29 March 1973
Birthplace: Emst, Holland
Joined club: 1997
Club League appearances: 32
Club League goals: 12
Last transfer fee: £5 million
Current estimated value: £7.5 million

Has shown a clean pair of heels to many a full-back since his arrival at Highbury, where his link with fellow countryman Dennis Bergkamp has proved fruitful for the Double winners. Seems a less than automatic choice for his country, though injury hampered his efforts in France '98 and he was most often introduced from the bench. A fleet-footed winger who can turn any game, he scored relatively rarely but spectacularly as in the 1998 FA Cup Final and the Charity Shield.

Emmanuel Petit

Plays for: Arsenal/France
Birthdate: 22 September 1970
Birthplace: Dieppe, France
Joined club: 1997
Club League appearances: 32
Club League goals: 2
Last transfer fee: £3.5 million
Current estimated value: £5 million

Having picked up Premiership, FA Cup and World Cup medals in one season, the future can only be an anti-climax for the Arsenal and France ace. Yet he retains a sense of perspective due to the loss of his brother. Plays effectively for club and country with the more defensively-minded Partick Vieira, each covering for the other as they advance to strike on goal: a spectacular third against Brazil was the icing on the cake.

Right: Sergio Conceicao of Portugal and Lazio. *Allsport*

Below : Emmanuel Petit slots home France's third in the World Cup Final. *David Leah/Allsport.*

Sergio Conceicao

Plays for: Lazio/Portugal
Birthdate: 15 November 1974
Birthplace: Coimbra, Portugal
Joined club: 1998
Last transfer fee: £6 million
Current estimated value: £6 million

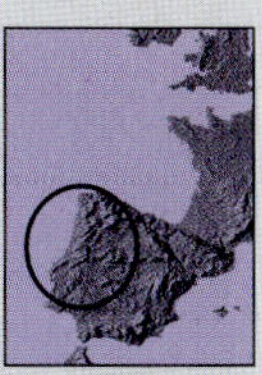

Conceicao's meteoric rise to stardom began in 1995, when he helped little Felgueiras gain promotion to the Portuguese First Division. They were relegated again the following season, but his talents as a dependable defender-cum-midfielder had caught the attention of FC Porto, who promptly snapped him up. Two successive domestic titles and a call-up to the national side later, Conceicao was ready to become the latest in a long line of Portuguese imports to Italy's Serie A.

Above: Paul Scholes celebrates after scoring against Tunisa. *Ben Radford/Allsport.*

Right: Dejan Stankovic collides with Kopke of Germany. *Clive Brunskill/Allsport.*

Paul Scholes

Plays for: Manchester United/England
Birthdate: 16 November 1974
Birthplace: Salford
Joined club: 1993
Club League appearances: 98
Club League goals: 26
Current estimated value: £7.25 million

A typical World Cup goal, created out of nothing, against Tunisia confirmed left-footed Paul Scholes as an automatic choice in any England team for the next half-dozen years. Blooded carefully by Alex Ferguson at Manchester United, he has both the skill and the temperament to emulate his hero Bobby Charlton for both club and country.

MIDFIELDERS

Dejan Stankovic

Plays for: Lazio/Yugoslavia
Birthdate: 11 September 1978
Birthplace: Belgrade, Yugoslavia
Joined club: 1998
Last transfer fee: £8 million
Current estimated value: £8 million

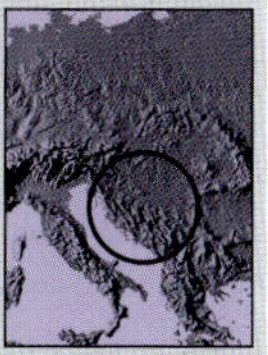

STANKOVIC

A product of Red Star Belgrade's famed academy of football, Stankovic was captain of the first team at 17. Two years later, Lazio scouts were at the Maracana stadium to watch him score a hat-trick. A lively, creative midfielder who loves to join the attack, he made his debut for Yugoslavia in April 1998 and claimed a goal in the World Cup against Germany – until replays showed he did not quite touch Predrag Mijatovic's cross.

Juan Veron

Plays for: Parma/Argentina
Birthdate: 9 March 1975
Birthplace: Buenos Aries, Argentina
Joined club: 1998
Last transfer fee: £11 million
Current estimated value: £11 million

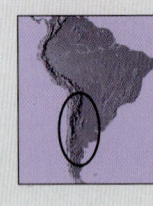

VERON

Known as 'Brujita', the largely unheralded Veron was many commentators' pick of the Argentine midfield in France '98. Has flourished in the finishing school of Serie A, first with Sampdoria and now Parma (where he joins fellow countryman Abel Balbo) with £2.25 million Roberto Sensini moving in the opposite direction. Links well with fellow Italian-based Simeone.

Above: Patrick Vieria of France and Arsenal. *Shaun Botterill/Allsport.*

Left: Agentinian Juan Sebastian Veron playing for Sampdoria in Serie A. *Claudio Villa/Allsport.*

Patrick Viera

Plays for: Arsenal/France
Birthdate: 23 June 1976
Birthplace: Dakar, Senegal
Joined club: 1996
Club League appearances: 64
Club League goals: 4
Last transfer fee: £4 million
Current estimated value: £4.5 million

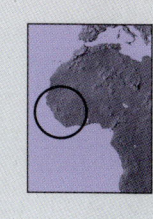

First signing of Arsène Wenger before he'd even warmed the Highbury hot seat, the African-born giant looks an unlikely midfielder at 6ft 3in, but uses those long legs to make timely interceptions and stride out towards the opponents' half, linking effectively with countryman Manu Petit.

Zinedine Zidane

Plays for: Juventus/France
Birthdate: 23 June 1972
Birthplace: Marseille, France
Joined club: 1996
Last transfer fee: £3.2 million
Current estimated value: £13 million

ZIDANE

'Zizou' was the undisputed star of France '98, even before he notched two goals in the showpiece Final. It was doubly sweet since the man on whom manager Jacquet had staked his reputation flopped in Euro '96, and to add a pair of untypical strikes – both headers from corners – was a bonus. On course to eclipse Platini as the all-time French footballing hero.

French hero Zinedine Zidane celebrates his second goal in the World Cup Finals. *Allsport.*

WORLD'S MOST VALUABLE PLAYERS
STRIKERS

Gabriel Batistuta

Plays for: Fiorentina/Argentina
Birthdate: 1 February 1969
Birthplace: Reconquista, Santa Fe
Joined club: 1991
Last transfer fee: £3.75 million
Current estimated value: £18 million

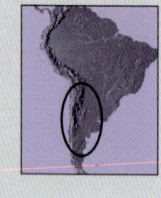

BATISTUTA

Established as a major goal machine in Italian football since moving from Boca Juniors in 1991, rumour had it that Batistuta wanted to try his hand in the Premiership. It hasn't happened – yet, anyway – but Argentina's all-time top scorer remains a feared figure. Returned to international contention in France '98 after manager Passarella ignored him while qualifying, and scored his fifth of the tournament against England in the second round.

Dennis Bergkamp

Plays for: Arsenal/Holland
Birthdate: 18 May 1969
Birthplace: Amsterdam, Holland
Joined club: 1996
Club League appearances: 90
Club League goals: 39
Last transfer fee: £7.5 million
Current estimated value: £12 million

Arsenal fans are well aware of the part Dennis Bergkamp played in bringing the Double to Highbury – and the fact that the club let Ian Wright go to let young Anelka grow under the Dutchman's tutelage proves the management know too! His success in the Premiership has now eclipsed his sad time with Inter Milan and brought him back to the heights he achieved with Ajax. Talking of heights, his aversion to flying is his only flaw.

Left: Gabriel Batistuta of Argentina and Fiorentina. *Mark Thompson/Allsport.*

Below: Dennis Bergkamp in a FA Carling Premiership match against Barnsley. *Clive Brunskill/Allsport.*

Oliver Bierhoff

Plays for: AC Milan/Germany
Birthdate: 1 May 1968
Birthplace: Karlsruhe, Germany
Joined club: 1998
Last transfer fee: £9 million
Current estimated value: £9 million

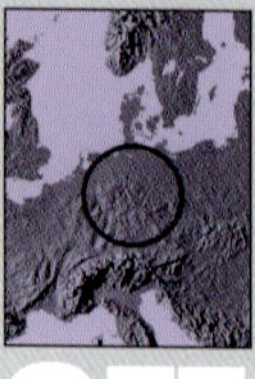

BIERHOFF

Ever-present alongside veteran Jürgen Klinsmann in France '98, 30 year-old Bierhoff crowned his summer with a move from Udinese to AC Milan. Not surprisingly, given his top-scorer status in Serie A, the fee was £9 million – and Germany, who owed much to six goals in the qualifying competition, clearly rate him just as highly.

Above: Pierluigi Casiraghi celebrates with Gianfranco Zola *Allsport.*

Left: Germany's Oliver Bierhoff. *Allsport.*

Pierluigi Casiraghi

Plays for: Chelsea/Italy
Birthdate: 4 March 1969
Birthplace: Monza, Italy
Joined club: 1998
Last transfer fee: £5.4 million
Current estimated value: £5.4 million

CASIRAGHI

Italy had been looking for an heir to Paolo Rossi – and Pierluigi Casiraghi eventually laid claim to the mantle after an uncertain start. Now, after five fruitful years at Lazio, he has the chance to impress in the Premiership, whence he was taken by Chelsea manager and former Juventus team-mate Vialli. Ignored in the World Cup, he has a point or two to prove.

Enrico Chiesa

Plays for: Parma/Italy
Birthdate: 29 December 1970
Birthplace: Verona, Italy
Joined club: 1996
Last transfer fee: £10 million
Current estimated value: £10 million

CHIESA

Signed from Cremonese in 1995, Chiesa set Sampdoria's Serie A campaign alight, finishing the league's third top scorer. Sadly, as with so many 'new Paolo Rossis', he couldn't keep it up after a big-money move to Parma, and despite equalising in his first international (under Sacchi) was only briefly in the picture as a sub when Maldini piloted Italy's fortunes in France '98. Still young enough to come again.

STRIKERS

Andy Cole

Plays for: Manchester United/England
Birthdate: 15 October 1971
Birthplace: Nottingham
Joined club: 1995
Club League appearances: 105
Club League goals: 46
Last transfer fee: £7 million
Current estimated value: £11 million

It must have been annoying for Andy Cole, after a 26-goal season, to hear his name bandied about as the makeweight in possible deals for other strikers. In reality Alex Ferguson values the man who became England's most expensive striker when moving from Newcastle in 1995. He misses a few, but gets in the position to do so – and further international recognition is far from beyond him as Hoddle gears up for Euro 2000.

Left: Parma's Enrico Chiesa. *Claudio Villa/Allsport.*

Below: Andy Cole in action for Manchester United. *Ross Kinnaird/Allsport.*

Kevin Davies

Plays for: Blackburn Rovers/England
Birthdate: 26 March 1977
Birthplace: Sheffield
Joined club: 1998
Last transfer fee: £7.25 million
Current estimated value: £7.25 million

DAVIES

The former Chesterfield teenager saw his value spiral tenfold when Roy Hodgson, impressed by his half-season in the Premiership with Southampton, splashed out to make him a Blackburn Rover. If he emulates Alan Shearer, who made a similar journey in 1992, the fleet-footed Davies will prove good value even for £7.25 million.

Right: Alessandro del Piero in action during the Champions League. *Clive Brunskill/Allsport.*

Below: Kevin Davies in his new Blackburn colours. *Allsport.*

Alessandro del Piero

Plays for: Juventus/Italy
Birthdate: 9 November 1974
Birthplace: Conegliano, Italy
Joined club: 1991
Current estimated value: £13 million

del PIERO

Rising fast from the shadow of Roberto Baggio when the ponytailed one moved to AC Milan in 1995, del Piero's goals took Juventus to the European Cup. Kept on the bench in Euro '96, he found injury hampering efforts to make a mark on the 1998 World Cup – but at 24 still had time on his side to notch more spectacular strikes.

Robbie Fowler

Plays for: Liverpool/England
Birthdate: 9 April 1975
Birthplace: Liverpool
Joined club: 1992
Club League appearances: 160
Club League goals: 92
Current estimated value: £6 million

FOWLER

The success of Michael Owen must have been hard for Robbie Fowler to swallow. Had injury not intervened in a spring 1998 Merseyside derby, he might have been partnering Alan Shearer in France. As it was, a meteoric career that had seen him bracketed with the likes of Keegan, Dalglish and Rush was halted in its tracks, to be picked up around Christmas 1998 when he'd have to push his 5ft 11in frame past Riedle and Dundee to occupy the striking place up for grabs alongside the new 'wonderboy'.

STRIKERS

Filippo Inzaghi

Plays for: Juventus/Italy
Birthdate: 9 August 1973
Birthplace: Bergamo, Italy
Last transfer fee: £9 million
Current estimated value: £9 million

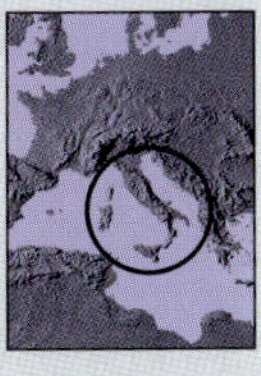

INZAGHI

The player Parma discarded in favour of Argentinian import Crespo was snapped up by Juve after an amazing season with Serie A newcomers Atalanta (he scored eight of their first ten goals of 1996-97, ending with 24 in 33). Inzaghi was capped against Brazil but featured only briefly as a substitute in France '98, where he'd been expected to partner club team-mate Allesandro del Piero up front.

Left: Robbie Fowler, Liverpool and England. *Allsport.*

Below: Filippo Inzaghi in Champions League action. *Gary Prior/Allsport.*

Patrick Kluivert

Plays for: Barcelona/Holland
Birthdate: 1 July 1976
Birthplace: Amsterdam, Holland
Last transfer fee: £10 million

KLUIVERT

Some may think he has an inflated opinion of himself, having turned down Manchester United and asked too much for Arsenal — but the fact is that Patrick Kluivert was desperately missed by the Dutch national side when sent off in France '98. His off-pitch dramas have further clouded the picture, but there's little doubt that aerial ability and good close control will make him a continuing threat wherever he chooses to play — provided he controls his temper.

Right: Yugoslavia's Predrag Mijatovic. *Allsport.*

Below: Patrick Kluivert celebrates after scoring for Holland. *Graham Chadwick/Allsport.*

Predrag Mijatovic

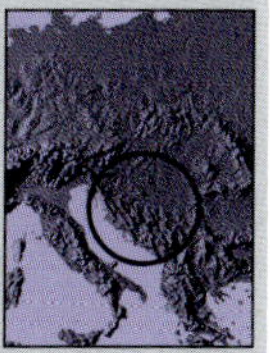

Plays for: Real Madrid/Yugoslavia
Birthdate: 19 January 1969
Birthplace: Podgorica, Yugoslavia
Joined club: 1996
Last transfer fee: £6.3 million
Current estimated value: £6.3 million

MIJATOVIC

Yugoslavia's top gun has made a formidable reputation during three seasons in Spain, firstly with Valencia – the unfashionable club whose runners-up position owed much to his goals – and latterly the legendary Real Madrid. At the Bernabeu he partnered Davor Suker, while internationally he links with Savicevic, and both would pay tribute to his invention.

81

Luis Oliveira

Plays for: Fiorentina/Belgium
Birthdate: 24 March 1969
Birthplace: Sao Paulo, Brazil
Joined club: 1996
Last transfer fee: £5 million
Current estimated value: £5 million

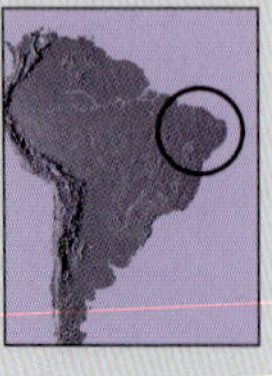

OLIVEIRA

Brazilian-born but raised in Brussels and granted Belgian citizenship, striker Oliveira is a product of the Anderlecht youth scheme who first rose to prominence with an 18-goal contribution to the club's 1990-91 Championship season. He has since been a consistent goalscorer in Italy for Cagliari and Fiorentina, but has sometimes struggled when playing for his adopted country – France '98 being a particularly difficult experience.

STRIKERS

Michael Owen

Plays for: Liverpool/England
Birthdate: 14 December 1979
Birthplace: Chester
Club League appearances: 38
Club League goals: 19
Current estimated value: £25 million

OWEN

The undisputed golden boy of the 1998 World Cup, Michael Owen rocketed from the substitutes' bench to stake a claim for international recognition. Having topped the domestic scoring lists in his first full season at Liverpool, this was no surprise to English critics, but they would be watching closely to see how he coped with the pressure to perform that he's now under. Speed and a stunning shot combine to make him a constant threat at any level.

Left: Luis Oliveria of Belguim. *David Cannon/Allsport.*

Below: Young England superstar Michael Owen in action for Liverpool. *Clive Brunskill/Allsport.*

Rivaldo

Plays for: Barcelona/Brazil
Birthdate: 19 April 1972
Birthplace: Recife, Brazil
Joined club: 1997
Last transfer fee: £8.5 million
Current estimated value: £14 million

RIVALDO

The surprise packet of Brazil's World Cup '98 bid, Rivaldo's two goals against Denmark and shoot-out strike in the drawn semi were arguably the most significant contribution of anyone in a yellow shirt. Ironically, on the club front he was signed by Barcelona from Deportivo in 1997 after a 21-goal season to replace national team-mate Ronaldo, but to be fair they signed Christophe Dugarry too. Both met in the 1998 Final, but the Frenchman had the last laugh.

Right: Superstar Ronaldo of Inter Milan and Brazil.
Clive Brunskill/Allsport.

Below: Rivaldo lines up for Brazil.
Mark Thompson/Allsport.

Ronaldo

Plays for: Inter Milan/Brazil
Birthdate: 22 September 1976
Birthplace: Rio de Janeiro
Joined club: 1997
Last transfer fee: £18 million
Current estimated value: £20 million

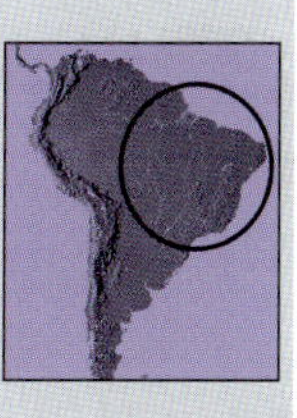

Sadly for the legendary Brazilian, his name is now inextricably linked with the 1998 World Cup Final for which he wasn't originally named, eventually played in and disappointed both himself and the watching world. Much will depend on whether he has the strength of character to overcome this and also the reaction of his team-mates: Roberto Carlos had earlier called him an individual rather than a team player.

Marcelo Salas

Plays for: Lazio/Chile
Birthdate: 24 December 1974
Birthplace: Temuco, Chile
Joined club: 1998
Last transfer fee: £15 million
Current estimated value: £15 million

SALAS

Top of Manchester United's shopping list for many months, Chile's biggest star seems happy to ply his trade in Serie A with Lazio, where he is expected to shine as brightly as in the World Cup. His double at Wembley in a February friendly earned him his 'Matador' nickname, and he added four in France to the 10 in 13 qualifying games. Look out Italian defences!

STRIKERS

Dejan Savicevic

Plays for: Fukuoki/Yugoslavia
Birthdate: 15 September 1966
Birthplace: Podgorica, Yugoslavia
Joined club: 1998
Current estimated value: £7.25 million

SAVICEVIC

Few players have been signed for £12 million and failed to get a game, but that was the fate of Dejan Savicevic when moving from Red Star Belgrade to AC Milan in 1992. Fourth in the queue for a striking berth, he bided his time and single-handedly won the 1994 European Cup for his club. Despite this, and a second round World Cup showing, he was now approaching 32 and had the incentive to show that his silky skills remain and he was far from over the hill despite being released by the San Siro outfit.

Left: Chilean Marcelo Salas of Parma. *Allsport*.

Below: Dejan Savicevic on international duty. *Allsport*.

Alan Shearer

Plays for: Newcastle United/England
Birthdate: 13 August 1970
Birthplace: Newcastle
Joined club: 1996
Club League appearances: 48
Club League goals: 27
Last transfer fee: £15 million
Current estimated value: £17 million

Britain's most expensive player has proved worth every penny of his fee, even though he has signally failed to enjoy domestic football's top prizes since returning to Tyneside, a Championship medal for Blackburn still his only silverware. 1998-99 must bring success or Shearer will depart for pastures new. Has ridden his injuries well, and remains a complete striker on the deck and in the air, even if his temperament has lately been questioned.

Below: Alan Shearer celebrates scoring against Argentina in the World Cup. *Ross Kinnaird/Allsport.*

Right: Davor Suker on top form during France 98. *Allsport.*

Davor Suker

Plays for: Real Madrid/Croatia
Birthdate: 1 January 1968
Birthplace: Osijek, Croatia
Joined club: 1996
Last transfer fee: £4 million
Current estimated value: £5.5 million

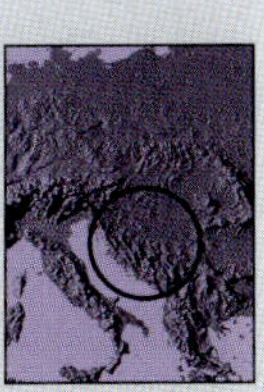

A triumphant World Cup for the old stager; even if he notched the last of his six goals in the third and fourth place play-off, the Golden Boot was his. Now entering his fourth decade, he brings every ounce of experience to bear whether for Croatia or Real Madrid, his second Spanish club. Creates as many goals as he scores, and is a handful for any defence.

Chris Sutton

Plays for: Blackburn Rovers/England
Birthdate: 10 March 1973
Birthplace: Nottingham
Joined club: 1994
Club League appearances: 113
Club League goals: 44
Last transfer fee: £5 million
Current estimated value: £7 million

The joint leading domestic striker of 1997-98 in England, Blackburn's Sutton is sadly certain never to add to his sole England cap while Glenn Hoddle is manager, having declined to play for the B team in the run-up to the World Cup. The former Norwich player is equally adept as central defender and striker, but few would consider playing him at the back when he poses such a threat both on the ground and in the air.

STRIKERS

Pierre van Hooijdonk

Plays for: Nottingham Forest/Holland
Birthdate: 29 November 1969
Birthplace: Steenbergen, Holland
Joined club: 1997
Club League appearances: 50
Club League goals: 30
Last transfer fee: £3 million
Current estimated value: £10 million

Unfortunately, having walked out on Nottingham Forest at the start of their 1998-99 Premiership return, the tall Dutchman has confirmed the opinion, voiced after a similar tactic was employed at Celtic, that though he has undoubted gifts he lacks team spirit. A fringe player in Dutch national terms, he scores more goals from set pieces than most forwards, and is handy in the air – but signing him is now a calculated risk.

Left: Blackburn's Chris Sutton in vocal mood.
Gary Prior/Allsport.

Below: Pierre van Hooijdonk. *Shaun Botterill/Allsport.*

Christian Vieri

Plays for: Lazio/Italy
Birthdate: 12 July 1973
Birthplace: Bologna, Italy
Last transfer fee: £18 million
Current estimated value: £25 million

Hotshot Christian Vieri preceded Filippo Inzaghi by moving from Atalanta to Juventus 12 months earlier, and was tempted away from the Italian champions when Atletico Madrid waved nearly £13 million in their direction. A double-figure goal tally followed as he sought to justify manager Raddy Antic's faith in him – though the club's form as a whole dwindled and he left for Lazio in 1998.

Below: Chritsian Vieri in a UEFA Cup quarter-final against Aston Villa. *Stu Forster/Allsport.*

Right: George Weah in action for AC Milan. *Claudio Villa /Allsport.*

George Weah

Plays for: AC Milan/Liberia
Birthdate: 1 October 1966
Birthplace: Monrovia, Liberia
Joined club: 1995
Last transfer fee: £5 million
Current estimated value: £7 million

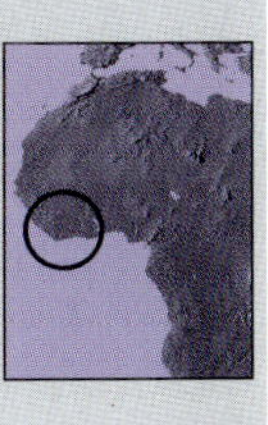

A legendary player and surely the most successful ever to emerge from his continent, Weah was the first African to carry off the European Footballer of the Year title. A move to AC Milan in 1995 followed several successive seasons in France for Monaco (under Arsène Wenger) and Paris Saint Germain, with whom he won every domestic honour. An all-round footballer whose powers have yet to wane as he approaches his mid-thirties.

Dwight Yorke

Plays for: Manchester United/Trinidad & Tobago
Birthdate: 3 November 1971
Birthplace: Canaan, Tobago
Joined club: 1998
Last transfer fee: £12.6 million
Current estimated value: £12.6 million

YORKE

Nippy forward converted from a winger to a central striker playing off a bigger man, Yorke enjoyed a fruitful relationship with first Savo Milosevic and then Stan Collymore at Villa, even if both players failed to hit peak form themselves — a point in Yorke's favour. After being pursued by Manchester United during the summer of 1998, Alex Ferguson finally got his man on deadline day for Champions' League qualification. Only time will tell if this was money well spent.

Below: Manchester United's new signing Dwight Yorke. *Ben Radford/Allsport.*

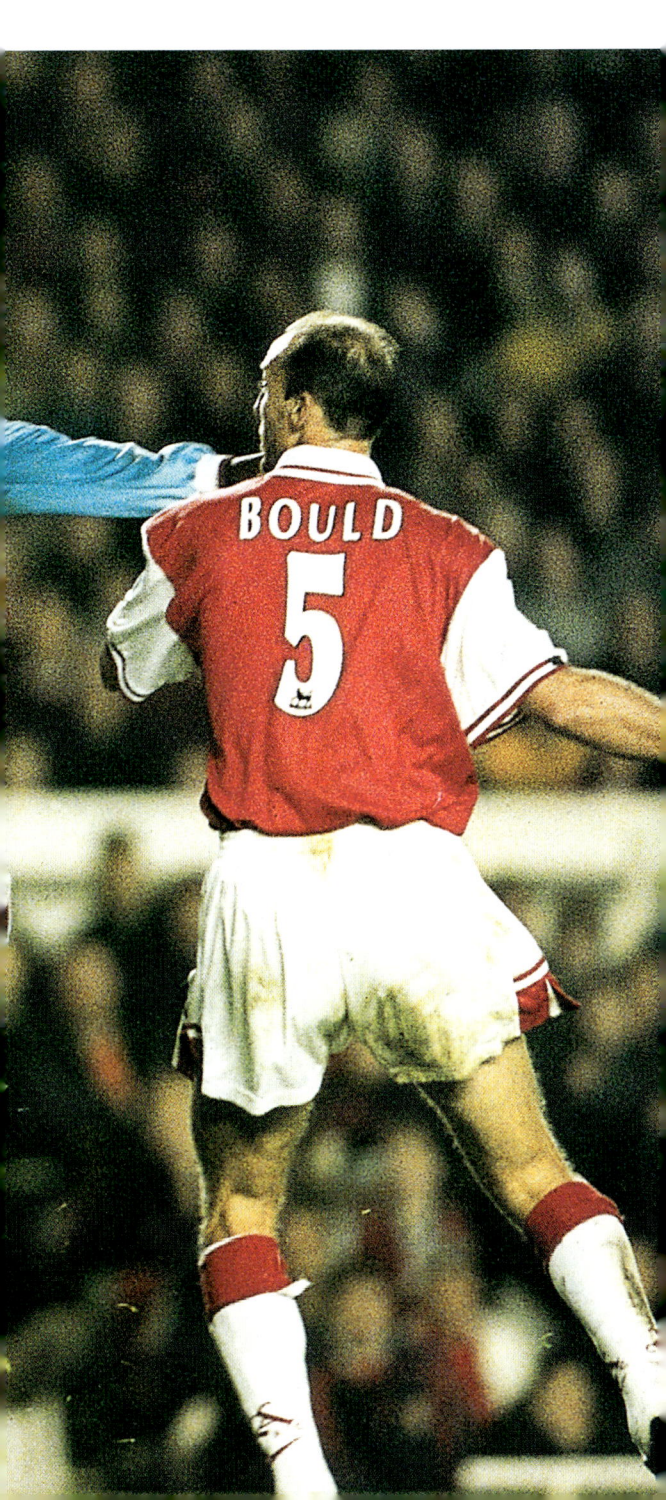

WORLD'S MOST VALUABLE PLAYERS INDEX

Fabien Barthez	6	Roberto Di Matteo	51
Jose Luis Chilavert	7	Ryan Giggs	52
Ruud Hesp	8	Giovanni	53
Kasey Keller	9	Jorg Heinrich	54
Gianluca Pagliuca	10	Paul Ince	55
Angelo Peruzzi	11	Juninho	56
Peter Schmeichel	12	Brian Laudrup	57
David Seaman	13	Steve McManaman	58
Steve Simonsen	14	Jay-Jay Okocha	59
Claudio Taffarel	15	Ariel Ortega	60
Edwin Van der Sar	16	Marc Overmars	61
Vitor Baia	17	Emmanuel Petit	62
Tony Adams	18	Sergio Conceicao	63
Slaven Bilic	19	Paul Scholes	64
Cafu	20	Dejan Stankovic	65
Sol Campbell	21	Juan Veron	66
Roberto Carlos	22	Patrick Viera	67
Frank de Boer	23	Zinedine Zidane	68
Marcel Desailly	24	Gabriel Batistuta	70
Rio Ferdinand	25	Dennis Bergkamp	71
Vegard Heggem	26	Oliver Bierhoff	72
Thomas Helveg	27	Pierluigi Casiraghi	73
Colin Hendry	28	Enrico Chiesa	74
Graeme Le Saux	29	Andy Cole	75
Frank Leboeuf	30	Kevin Davis	76
Paolo Maldini	31	Alessandro del Piero	77
Miguel Angel Nadal	32	Robbie Fowler	78
Nourredine Naybet	33	Filipo Inzaghi	79
Gary Neville	34	Patrick Kluivert	80
Arthur Numan	35	Pedrag Mijatovic	81
Dan Petrescu	36	Luis Oliveira	82
Tomas Repka	37	Micheal Owen	83
Gareth Southgate	38	Rivaldo	84
Jaap Stam	39	Ronaldo	85
Moreno Torricelli	40	Marcelo Salas	86
Taribo West	41	Dejan Savicevic	87
Christian Wörns	42	Alan Shearer	88
David Beckham	44	Davor Suker	89
Rui Costa	45	Chris Sutton	90
Edgar Davids	46	Pierre van Hooijdonk	91
Ronald de Boer	47	Christian Vieri	92
Ivan de la Peña	48	George Weah	93
Denilson	49	Dwight Yorke	94
Didier Deschamps	50		